Poems Of Wonder

Edited By Lynsey Evans

First published in Great Britain in 2024 by:

Young Writers
Remus House
Coltsfoot Drive
Peterborough
PE2 9BF
Telephone: 01733 890066
Website: www.youngwriters.co.uk

Book Design by Ashley Janson

Softback ISBN 978-1-83565-421-7
Printed and bound in the UK by BookPrintingUK
Website: www.bookprintinguk.com
YB0590H

CONTENTS

St Paul's CE Junior School, Barrow-In-Furness

Jacob Howard (10) 52
Alicia Charlton (10) 53
Jazlyn Lee (10) 54
Evan Coburn (11) 55
Lucas Brennan (10) 56
Ameena Miah (11) 57
Xander Rayney (10) 58
Oscar Rowland (10) 59
Georgia Royle (11) 60
Noah Olliver (11) 61
Hallie Thomas (11) 62
Hollie Bell (10) 64
Scarlett Parkinson (11) 65
Lilly Keogh (10) 66
Penny Brough (10) 67
Jess Renshaw (10) 68
Carter Deakin (10) 69
Elicia Thompson (10) 70
Zebulon Morrison (10) 71
Georgia-Mae Frazer (11) 72
Rosie Peel (10) 73
Hadley Hill (10) 74

Warren Farm Primary School, Kingstanding

Favour Ndikum (8) 75
Evie Gouldingay (10) 76
Harry Davies (8) 78
Maison Crofts (10) 80
Thiciane Alynne Junqueira De Andrade (9) 81
Hope Matangwe (9) 82
Hollie Treharne (9) 83
Maiya Ceesay (9) 84
Abdullateef Ayantola (9) 85
Olivia Nottingham (9) 86
Lexi Barmer (8) 87
Harley Bree (8) 88
Bobby Nottingham (9) 89
YaXin Wang (10) 90
Amelia Bravington-Bryant (8) 91
Harry Martin (7) 92
Emmanuel Sambayi (9) 93
Modesireoluwa Soyannwo 94
Cameron Orbell (9) 95
Arlo Martin (7) 96
Destiny Clayton (10) 97

Whirley Primary School, Macclesfield

Luke Pateman (7) 98
Bobby Villers (8) 100
Lucas Scott (11) 101
Lilliana Millward (10) 102
Esme Cope (10) 103
Amara Lamptey-Spencer (7) 104
Holly Delaney (9) 105
Max Handley (8) 106
Isabelle Hibberts (11) 107
Ava McClelland (8) 108
Olive McGillivray (8) 109
Jacob Eaton (9) 110
Arthur Gerrard (8) 111
Charlie Macey (8) 112
Will Heywood (9) 113
Evie Ashcroft (7) 114
Flynn Simister (8) 115
Max Joseph Brown (10) 116
Bella Heyes (8) 117
Rory Owen (7) 118
Oliver Pateman (10) 119
Nola Campbell (10) 120
Jasper Bains (10) 121
Erin Tench (9) 122
Ellie Norbury (10) 123
Eliza Utteridge (8) 124
Millie Harrad (10) 125
Aiden Choi (8) 126
Beth Shaul (7) 127
Isaac Cockburn (11) 128
Mia Scragg (10) 129
Matilda Naughton (8) 130
Emily Stewart (8) 131

Molly Macey (11) 132
Lola Rowson (8) 133
Isla Mather (8) 134
Elijah Cockburn (7) 135
Ella Scragg (8) 136
Eliza White (9) 137
Oliver Stuart (8) 138
Harry Hibberts (9) 139
Jack Robson (8) 140
Rosa Lampley Spencer (7) 141
Coen Beech (9) 142
Matthew W (10) 143
Maria Morgan (9) 144
Matthew Cain (9) 145
Anson Choi (10) 146
Connor Casey (8) 147
Jessica Hooley (9) 148
Ashley Foster (10) 149
Riley Scragg (8) 150
Isaac Jackson (8) 151
Niamh Lee (9) 152
Isabelle Whitehead (10) 153
Paddy Considine (10) 154
Samuel Mather (11) 155
Eve Lewis (10) 156
Spencer Davies (7) 157

Ysgol Gynradd Gymunedol Gymraeg Llantrisant, Miskin

Hari Griffiths (10) 158
Freya Parry (11) 159
Celyn Stephens (11) 160
Osian Williams (11) 161
Mari Jones (11) 162
Lucas Gilligan (10) 163
Molly Wheel (11) 164
Kienan Noble (11) 165
Kimmi Kenny (11) 166

THE POEMS

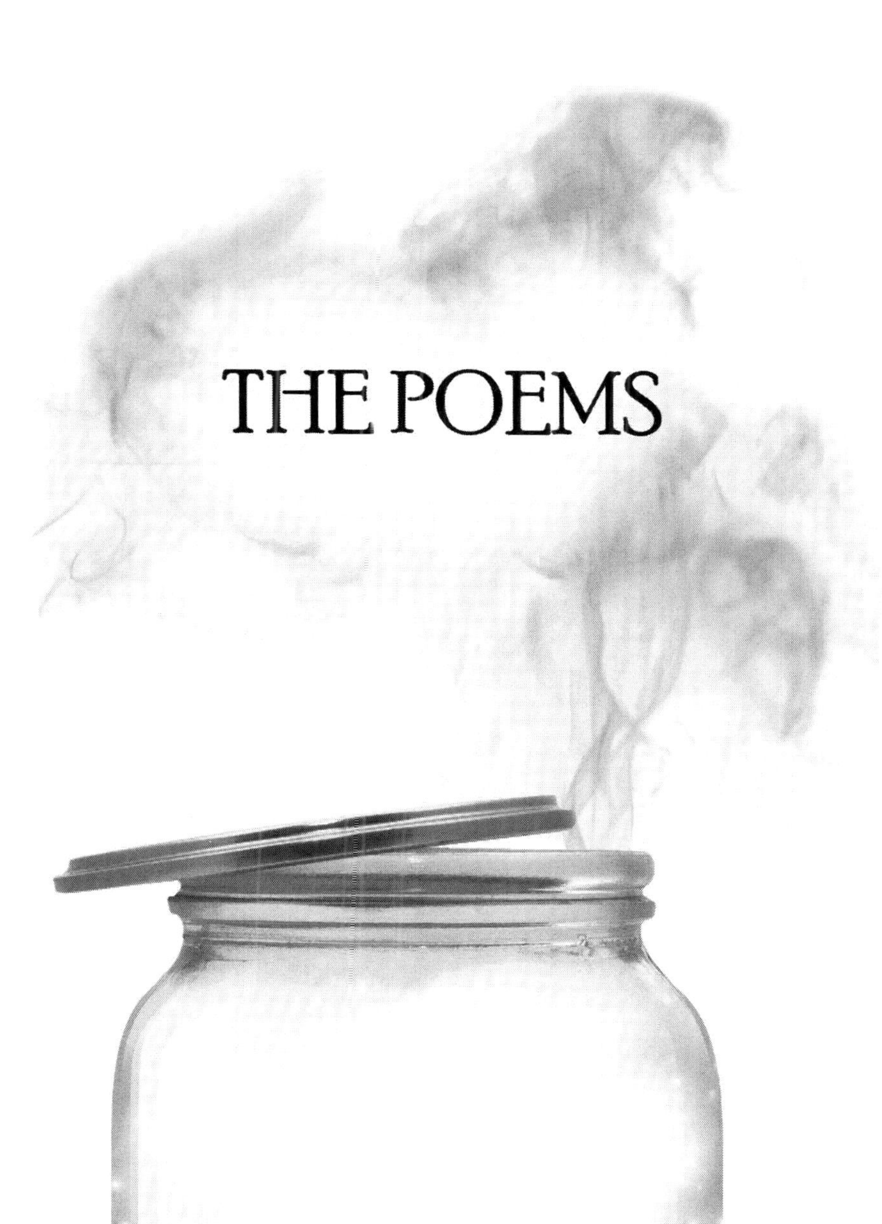

The Raven Of Death

The Raven appears and your heart shakes.
It's standing by the silent lake.
The Raven is a ghost of our past,
And Raven says, "Time goes fast."

Raven carried a rose, tight in his beak,
And finally said, "This world is bleak."
Raven told me to take the rose
And I would go to Heaven with a fabulous pose.

I refused to take it, for I couldn't die yet.
And Raven jumped into the river to get wet.
Raven came back out of the river
And my heart began to shiver.

He shook the water over me,
Then said, "Trust me, you'll be free!"
I took the rose and began to fly,
For I had probably died.

I let go of the rose and fell back down.
I was still alive in this town.
I won't stay in this world,
I feel like a golden crown...

Eva Carr (11)
Bere Alston Primary School, Bere Alston

The Voice

The moonlit sky shone brightly across the empty churchyard.
The owl screeched like a nail on a chalkboard.
The wind howled like a pack of wolves.
The branches tossed as if they were alive.
Suddenly, I heard a voice, a voice like no other.
The voice said...

"This following path will lead you to death.
This following path will lead you to the end.
This following path will lead to your demise.
This following path will lead you to eternal unhappiness.
This following path will lead you to death... death... death!"

Such a strange message it was -
A message like a warning, a warning of my demise.
Argh! I was dead but still alive.
I was in another land. The land of hell!
And so, with it all gone I chanted...

The following path led me to Hell,
To the end, to my demise,
To my unhappiness, to my death!

Max Magner (10)
Bere Alston Primary School, Bere Alston

Runaway

My hair floated in the rainy wind,
My eyes getting watery from my sin.

I could no longer be in the possession of the king,
I feel so free in the forest, the birds sing.

My pleasing pink quilted dress,
No longer pleasant I must confess.

I cried tears of pure joy,
To know I was no longer being controlled like a toy.

Little did they know, I was two steps ahead,
I wasn't sleeping peacefully in my bed.

A free bird, no longer trapped in a cage,
Now it's time to turn the next page.

They can't catch me now,
They can't catch me now.

Poppy Babb (11)
Bere Alston Primary School, Bere Alston

My Superpowers

Not everyone has powers, not many at all,
I can fly. Don't worry, I won't fall.
Shape-shifting, mind reading, teleporting.
But, of all the powers I have,
My favourite is flying, overall.
Every night, when the stars are bright,
I sneak out, taking in the beautiful sights.
People see me, wherever they are,
But don't know what, or perhaps who, I am,
But no, it isn't a scam.

Dan Browne (10)
Bere Alston Primary School, Bere Alston

Cannibal's Victim

C arefully seeking me,
A nd escapes.
N ever once seen him before,
N ot something I will ever wish for.
I naudible, it caught up to me,
B aring its grip,
A ddressing me, a victim,
L uring me closer.

H ell is where I am,
E nsuring no escape.
L eading me to fate,
P eering over the bait.

Lexi-Leigh Sherman (10)
Bere Alston Primary School, Bere Alston

The Astronaut

A s quick as a cheetah, the spaceship flew up,
S ilently the other ships say, "What is up?"
T ON618 may approach,
R est of the spaceship smells like a cockroach,
O bjects flying into the unknown,
N ever-ending hoop of stars that just seem to clone,
A liens and
U FOs,
T hat is what nobody knows.

Jasper Ayres (10)
Bere Alston Primary School, Bere Alston

Nightmare

N ight-time,
I t will scare you.
G o back to sleep,
H ope you don't wake up,
T hey all say.
M ight be good,
A nd will always be bad,
R ight now go to sleep,
E very night.

Macy Abbott (10)
Bere Alston Primary School, Bere Alston

The Spectacular Unicorns

U nicorns are fun
N othing you can do
I ntelligent
C reatures
O riginal too
R unning
N ear to you.

Sophie Symons (10)
Bere Alston Primary School, Bere Alston

Ghosts

G houls screeching
H orrible screams
O minous presence
S omething lurking
T errifying beasts
S omeone near.

Rhys Richardson (11)
Bere Alston Primary School, Bere Alston

Life To Death Of A Sapling

In a faraway land, on a hill,
There lay trees, sisters and brothers,
Among the adults, was a sapling very still,
On the ground, lay rubbish and abandoned plastic covers.

All it ever saw was insects flying around over her shoulder,
As the days went by, the sapling noticed something peculiar,
It was evolving, becoming bigger and taller,
As hours, days and months went by, it became an adult.

Inside, it still had no bones,
Yet as time passed by, it became winter,
It saw its friends crying over lost pinecones,
As night falls once again, a human is stabbed by a splinter.

Winter passed away and spring gave life,
The newly grown saw a group of humans who seemed shy,
In the middle of spring flowers bloomed filling the Earth with happiness,
If it could, it would shed a tear, tears would fly.

Finally one of the flowers changed into a scrumptious peach.
Once flowers all turned they would fall, rattling.
They had colours like sand on the beach,
Containing seeds which will one day give birth to a newborn sapling.

Roshan M Asruf (8)
Birkbeck Primary School, Sidcup

Tropical Dragon Island

My family and I travelled over the shining sea,
Arriving at an island, we felt free,
We walked across the hot, white, sandy beach,
We headed into a jungle, on the floor we saw a lonely peach.
We were so hungry, but we had the one peach to share,
As we headed deeper into the jungle, we saw a bright flare,
Investigating, we saw a fire-spurting dragon,
We glanced across and found the reason.
A large, fearsome dinosaur was hurtling towards us,
We all ran back towards our boat, all becoming breathless,
Could we escape these magnificent creatures?
Could we reach the water?
Bang! There behind us, a massive explosion,
We made it to the ocean,
But the dragon and T-rex were inches away,
We started up the boat, would we escape, or were we prey?
We let out an almighty scream,
Suddenly, there I awoke in my room and realised it was all a dream.

Carter Kelly (9)
Birkbeck Primary School, Sidcup

Time Travelling

At night me and my brother see a time machine
We step in wondering what will be seen
I take a glance at the big bright sea
And then a Viking says to me
"Who are you?"
"Do you want some poison stew?"
We run back to our machine
And find the sight of an Egyptian queen
Pyramids loom over our head
How we see the desert spread
Servants work day and night
As kids play with their kites
We go back to our device
And see a T-rex, but do not look twice
We run and run back to our contraption
And leave the dinosaur with a big reaction.

Ayla Saeed (8)
Birkbeck Primary School, Sidcup

Magical Fame

While I stride down the pathway,
Cute little cottages on either side lay,
Small children squeal with delight,
Before hurrying away as though I might bite,
Further on, a group of adults stand,
When I walk by, they bow low as though I am in a band,
Some plead to try my latest invention,
So I explain how it stops all the tension,
How it makes your life really easy,
By speeding things up, so they don't get queasy,
I continue on along my way,
Feeling proud and happy on this fine day,
Magic swirls around my bed,
While everyone cheers inside my head.

Maya Majithia (9)
Birkbeck Primary School, Sidcup

Holiday

In my favourite dream
I scream
I'm far away, on holiday.

Me and my siblings
Go down the water slide
While we glide
We're side by side.

I make friends with the animation team
Me and my siblings beam
Everyone goes on the camels, except for me
I go on a horse
Where I see my family
Where I see the sunset.

We hurry home
Back to the rain
It feels like a hurricane
Compared to a holiday.

Jessica Ward (8)
Birkbeck Primary School, Sidcup

Jungle

J ungle friends join me in my dreams
U nder my duvet all warm and cosy, my pig friend joins me all pink and rosy
N othing stops us from having a blast, running and racing through rainforests really fast
G iggling and swinging with monkeys in the trees
L iving the dream as I sit by a stream
E yes open as the sun slowly rises, I can't wait for tonight when my animal friends and I reunite.

Betsy E (9)
Birkbeck Primary School, Sidcup

Best Time

Underneath the starry, sleepy sky
Lorie starts to drift off to sleep
She dreams of stories about the moon
And the moon whispers, "Sleep little one."

Lorie rests her mind on a beautiful ride through bright lights
She snugs and hugs her toys
As the boys in the other room snore
They dream of a dinosaur's roar
I hope you enjoyed the night-time ride.
Bye-bye.

Siena Lean (8)
Birkbeck Primary School, Sidcup

Otis Potter

H e walked, walked through the dark, gloomy corridors,
O wls twit-twooed as the man came in,
G hosts suddenly came through the castle walls,
W inged bats flew overhead,
A s he performed a mouth-opening spell,
R ats rumbled across the creaking floor,
T hen his eyes twitched as...
S leep left him and he woke up to the bright sun.

Otis Pope (8)
Birkbeck Primary School, Sidcup

The Mystical Castle

The mystical castle lives far in the woods,
Hidden in the trees like a puzzle that is unsolvable.
This castle is bold with green vines crawling up its front.
Inside this castle lies a staircase that leads to a secret passageway.
Inside this passageway is a secret room with a treasure chest.
Within this chest lies your wildest dreams.
No one will ever find this castle or chest... until now!
A girl called April was on a walk in the woods and came across the castle.
She went inside and found the room with the chest inside.
She opened the chest and her face shone with a gleam.
It was like all her dreams and wishes came to life!
She told all her friends and family and decided to make the castle her new home.
She decorated it with lights as bright as the sun and chairs as soft as clouds.
They cleaned the castle to make it as if it was just built.
Over the years each explorer that would find the chest would make the castle their home.

Naomi Bidder (10)
Central Primary School, Port Talbot

The Magical Secret Night Garden

Once upon a dream,
I walked through a magical door.
There were sparkles and glitter
In a magical secret night garden.
Birds were glancing and dancing
In the magical clouds.
I was excited and scared;
Sadly, I was on my own.
Crying in front of a sunset
With sunset colours, stripy and clean.
As I slept in my bed,
Thinking about what was in my head...
It was easy and clear:
I felt fear, like a dog in a cage!
Was it my imagination?
Was it real or was it a dream?
Full of fear, I could think clearly;
It was all a dream.
It wasn't so real.

Lace Evans (10)
Central Primary School, Port Talbot

Jungle Dream

I have a dream I am on a path,
Surrounded by trees as tall as a giraffe.
The chirps and trills of bugs and creatures,
This jungle I'm in has so many features.
To my left, beetles are crawling,
From the canopy above, butterflies falling.
The bark of the trees, hard like a turtle's shell,
A scent of bright tropical flowers I smell.
The screech of monkeys swinging above,
To the right I see colourful parrots in love.
I suddenly wake up alone in my bed,
But the wonderful jungle will stay in my head.

Kian Morgan (9)
Central Primary School, Port Talbot

Girls Love Football Too

Girls can be princesses,
Girls can be cool,
But I'd much rather be kicking a ball.

We play together,
We are a team,
Football has always been my dream.

I love hearing the cheers and the roars,
It makes my heart pound,
Every time my team scores.

So next time you boys think you're better than me,
Go grab a ball,
And we will see.

I may look sweet, I may look pretty,
I'll always be better,
And you will never beat me!

Tayleanna Mattock-Westlake (9)
Central Primary School, Port Talbot

Farm Dream

It was a dark, stormy night
I had a fight in my mind.
Went to sleep with my cosy sheep,
Then I saw on my arm a big farm.
Horses, pigs, rabbits, cows
They all did a bow.
One pig had wings and flew out of my dream.
Rabbit squeaks, chicken runs,
I can only hear the drums.
Then my sheep screams, *beep, beep*
I woke up in the car
In the middle of a bar.

Emma Guszczak (9)
Central Primary School, Port Talbot

Adventure Dreamer

In my dreams late at night,
Pirates came to steal and fight,
They caged me in steel and dragged me away,
To an island called Misery Bay,
They threw me into a cave where torches shone bright,
What I saw gave me a tremendous fright,
Pirates running, ready to fight,
It took all my courage but I tried as I might,
I defeated the pirates and walked into the light.

Josh Lewis (9)
Central Primary School, Port Talbot

A Perfect Day

The sun was brightly shining,
Everyone was smiling,
A sign for Anna Maria Island caught my eye,
Way up high I saw birds in the sky,
The sea and the sand,
Go hand in hand.

We went to a cute little cafe,
It was a great part of the day,
We got snow cones,
We both had our own,
Suddenly I woke to find I was at home in my bed.

Halle Smith (10)
Central Primary School, Port Talbot

Strange Stormy Sky

In my dreams last night,
There were shining stars in the night,
I flew past the moonlight,
Like the sun in summer,
Many horses and drummers,
I screamed with creeping cheers,
I had to face my frightening fears,
I had butterflies in my head,
When I woke up from bed.

Toshani Roy (9)
Central Primary School, Port Talbot

Dreams

D own in my dream jungle
R umbling racing gorilla had a fungus
E dward was his name, as you know
A nd he was very ill, he was going to throw
M aybe he will be as good as before
S eriously, he was below.

Suvarthi Mondal (8)
Central Primary School, Port Talbot

Wish Upon A Star

Once upon a dream,
There was a beautiful gleam,
I lean closer as it drifts away,
It's like an illusion,
Colourful and dark,
Bright and light,
Like the stars,
Up in the sky,
Hoping for a dream,
That will be seen.

Freddie Houghton (8)
Central Primary School, Port Talbot

Fun Times

By doing what you love,
By caring about another,
By meeting someone new,
Can make you realise you had fun.

Olivia Monaghan (10)
Central Primary School, Port Talbot

The Survivor Of Death

I woke up in fear
Feeling like I could disappear
It was a very dark abyss
I could not dismiss
It was very dark and I was terrified
Nothing to see, I looked from side to side
It stamped its ninety-nine feet
It made my brain think it was very steep
Sad that I may die
I looked up high into the sky
The crash was very heavy
Good thing I landed safely
I looked along the planet
It looked like a very bad habit
Crumbled houses and smashed towers
I wandered around for hours and hours
I saw something appear
It made me scream in tears
Screaming loud
My dog howled
It was a dream!

Darwin Hopkins (8)
Dolphinholme CE Primary School, Dolphinholme

Daisy And Evil Vel

I fell from the sky and I saw a magical forest with
smoke floating and fireflies in jars guiding the way.
I walked through the forest and I saw a magical horse,
I gently approached her.
Suddenly I hopped on her.
I called her Daisy, I felt so happy but I saw something
following me,
It was Evil Vel.
She wanted to kill all the magical horses, especially
Daisy.
I felt brave and strong because we were going to
defeat Evil Vel.
Suddenly Daisy blasted Evil Vel with poisonous magical
horse poo.
She fell to the ground and disappeared.
Before I knew it I was back in my bed.

Darcy Clegg (8)
Dolphinholme CE Primary School, Dolphinholme

Candy Land

One starry little night all blooming and bright,
I looked at the picture hanging on my wall,
I gazed up at the stars and I started to float,
I whirled towards the picture,
I shouted for help as I was floating into my picture...

When I arrived I leapt into candyfloss,
I saw Grandpa sitting in his wonky chair,
I leapt and said, "Hello!"

Sparkles and marshmallows drifted from the sky,
A ballerina said I could stay,
I said, "Yes!"
She showed me her moves,
I danced with joy.

And that was the end of Candy Land.

Flora Haxby (7)
Dolphinholme CE Primary School, Dolphinholme

One Snowy Night

O nce upon a night-time
N aughty children in the bed
E verybody sound asleep

S tars in the night sky
N obody playing in the snow
O wls flying by in the tree
W indows closed to keep out the cold
Y awning loudly when they go to sleep

N aughty children creep downstairs
I n their pyjamas and slippers
G etting food out of the fridge
H e looked out of the window
T ell everybody it is snowing.

Lucas Camplin (8)
Dolphinholme CE Primary School, Dolphinholme

Amazing Adventures

Once upon a dream,
I sit by a flowing stream,
With my cat on my lap,
My friend Vanessa and my mum tell me I need to wear a hat.
And sister, Riah, Harry, Hermionie by my side,
We all are smiling with great pride,
We look at the woods which look pretty good,
Until we go inside!
We all stop smiling with great pride,
Because we get kidnapped by a poisonous snake,
Then it opens its enormous mouth,
I'm really scared, but then I wake,
To find I am at home in my bed instead.

Thea Edwards (8)
Dolphinholme CE Primary School, Dolphinholme

Candy Canes Land

C andy canes are everywhere, all the trees are made of them,
A funny-looking reindeer comes over with candy cane horns,
N ever have I seen such a beauty before,
D ancing in the forest, trying every one,
Y awning and sleepy, I come to a break,

L ying on the floor looking at the view,
A nd the weird-looking birds too,
N ext morning I decide to dream a bit more,
D ying to hear more, I wake up and am ready to continue next time.

Pippa Cunningham (9)
Dolphinholme CE Primary School, Dolphinholme

Magic Fest

I closed my eyes and this is what I saw, sparkles, dragons and so much more!
I was with my koala clinging as tight as can be.
Sweets, stars, fairies and unicorns were dancing and singing beautiful songs.
Stalls were everywhere selling magic bottles and magic sweets too.
There was magic everywhere, we danced on clouds and sang songs.
Fireflies danced to the songs.
But when it finished I closed my eyes and I saw my bedroom right in front of me.

Amy Torr (8)
Dolphinholme CE Primary School, Dolphinholme

Lasagna

L asagna, imagine that
A s big as a mountain
S crumdiddlyumptious it could be
A bnormal that would be
G iant buildings as tall as can be like the Leaning Tower of Pizza!
N ext, what happens, I take a bite and I find myself behind bars. But I take another bite out of the bars and yum, I am free!
A lasagna comes up to me and we become friends but I eat him in the end.

Laurence Au Benedetto (8)
Dolphinholme CE Primary School, Dolphinholme

Clowns

C aught in a cave with millions of clowns, just sitting there waiting to be found,
L ost, looking for an exit, petrified and scared,
O r is that an exit over there? Oh no, it's a bear!
W ill I ever leave these spooky characters?
N o exit to be found, but then I found to be,
S uddenly, I woke up in my bed; no harm had been done, no characters, no clowns, just me and my mum.

Mabel Frenell-Hey (9)
Dolphinholme CE Primary School, Dolphinholme

Football

F ootball is the best ball game.
O n the pitch there are two brilliant players, Ronaldo and Mbappé.
O n the pitch, nothing can stop them.
T eam game.
B est friends: Laurence and a cute cat.
A ll the cats are mine.
L aurence likes Mbappé and I like Ronaldo.
L ots of food.

Nick Akimov (8)
Dolphinholme CE Primary School, Dolphinholme

The Dragons

I could see dragons flying around my window,
And a dragon came flying into my house.
Argh! What the mac 'n' cheese was that?
I went downstairs and saw a dragon,
Lying on the kitchen floor.

Edward (7)
Dolphinholme CE Primary School, Dolphinholme

I Want To Live In Japan

I want to live in Japan,
And I want to use a pan for pancakes,
And I want to eat a cake with my friends,
And I want to make new friends,
And I want a best friend and a special friend,
And I want to be favourite friend with you,
And the next day more pancakes!
More cake!
More friends!
Pizza for lunch and for tea the next day,
Drink!
Play Nintendo, Xbox, PlayStation,
Then go to the park,
Play and swim,
Football, tennis, golf, volleyball, cricket,
Play with cousin, Mum, Dad, grandads, nannas, brothers, stepsister,
Play Cluedo and carve pumpkins.

Tate Curran (8)
Mabe Community Primary School, Mabe

100 Million

The ground is as green as an emerald.
The sky is as blue as lapis lazuli.
The house is filled with riches,
It is made out of gold for the walls,
Diamonds for the roof and iron for the doors.
The path is emerald.
Banging is coming from a room.
100 million is coming soon.
A timer is shaking as he is shouting.
A car comes by as he is carrying a prize.
A knock on the door as a surprise,
A play button is here finally for me.

Bowe Saberton (9)
Mabe Community Primary School, Mabe

Horseland Is My Dream

It's pretty in Horseland,
Horses gallop across the meadow as foals lie on the tickly grass,
I look around, I see it all,
I hear birds chirping their song,
Horses neigh,
I smell the nice smell of daffodils,
It's calm and peaceful there.
As the sun sets on Horseland,
Horses nestle beneath the swaying tree,
It looks like it is waving,
My heart is happy as I am surrounded by horses.

Evvie Bolton (9)
Mabe Community Primary School, Mabe

I Want To Be A Palaeontologist

I want to be a palaeontologist,
I want to make history.
I want to own a museum,
Like the Colosseum.
To find a diplodocus,
And never lose focus.
I will be a palaeontologist.

It will feel like I'm in an endless veil,
If I ever fail.
But I'll always follow my dream,
So I'll succeed.
I will be a palaeontologist.

Lucas Gates (9)
Mabe Community Primary School, Mabe

Land Of Heaven

Balls whistling over the food stands,
Heading straight for your head,
Music playing by different bands,
People jumping into their beds.

Restaurants scattered everywhere,
People going to shops and getting buns,
Great animals, such as bears,
Everybody is having fun!

Locryn Trezise (9)
Mabe Community Primary School, Mabe

Land Of Footballs

Balls whistling through the air,
Goals are going everywhere,
With a crowd like the size of a fair,
People bicycle-kicking here and there.
Men eating and getting ready for the big game,
Harry Kane getting the fame.

Charlie Pellow (9)
Mabe Community Primary School, Mabe

My Jungle

In the jungle it's fun,
The rhino weighs a ton.

A bird whistles,
As the great big thistle grows.

The sun beams through the air,
Monkeys rip and tear.

Hector Knowles (8)
Mabe Community Primary School, Mabe

Shooting Stars

Stars shooting,
Meteors moving,
The galaxy glides,
The clouds are grey as clay,
It went black,
The moon stopped twinkling,
The fire went out,
Awoo!

Arlow French (9)
Mabe Community Primary School, Mabe

Autumn Dreams

Awesome autumn under the trees,
Lives the handsome hedgehog,
Using leaves for a murky burrow,
And no one knows about them.

Mason Carter (8)
Mabe Community Primary School, Mabe

Excellent Autumn

D igging hedgehogs
R emind me of
E xcellent autumn,
A wesome autumn,
M uddy autumn.

Zaak Boots (8)
Mabe Community Primary School, Mabe

The Chicken Gods' Palace

The walls were quartz.
The doors were bronze,
And the pillars were gold,
Like the sun in summer.

Stanley Nelmes (8)
Mabe Community Primary School, Mabe

The Pirate God

An unknown thing soaring up in the sky,
While we're down on Earth eating a pie.
Me and Sebastian hear something above,
My friend glances up; it is a snow-white dove.
Heading outside, we see something move,
We hear someone singing, getting into the groove.
"Hallelujah, hallelujah," it trills to us boys,
Is it Pirate God? Maybe he can explain all the noise.
Pirate God then says, "We need your help,"
To which, we let out a yelp.
The two of us ask, "We have to aid you?"
Pirate God says, "Please come and don't argue."
We need to get up to Heaven as fast as can be,
As the clock turns eleven, just wait and see.
We'll teleport there as the ship has sank,
All crew members ordered to walk the plank!
Do as I say and none will, and have lots of fun,
For when you wake up, the dream will be done!

Jacob Howard (10)
St Paul's CE Junior School, Barrow-In-Furness

On The Cheese Planet

In a fantasy, on a warm, toasty night,
I open my eyes, and am given a fright!
I float on my back in a sizzling sea,
Turning over, I realise it's as yellow as can be!
There are creatures waiting on the edges,
Hiding nervously behind star-silver hedges.
Strange languages they speak,
Past them, I try my best to sneak.
Donkey fairies fluttering flamingo-pink,
Friendly see-through snakes, off with a slink.
Eating starry bushes and drinking pure moonlight,
Never has there been such a crazy night!
I peer across mozzarella rivers, looking around,
They're frolicking; making a noisy sound.
Parmesan rains down from the sky,
It may seem false, but be assured; it's not a lie!
This planet is cheese,
Houses, people and trees!
To eat moonlight and stars may seem untrue,
But in a dream, it might happen to you!

Alicia Charlton (10)
St Paul's CE Junior School, Barrow-In-Furness

Ginger Queen

I walk down with my other ginger pal,
When littles come down and sing a song,
When they come I almost fall,
They grab me, their grip so strong,
We fly high, higher than the sky,
They let go, we land where only ginger people go,
There we see the fairies wave goodbye,
As we go where only ginger people know,
Me and my ginger pal get grabbed again,
They take us to the Ginger Queen,
She's a pretty lady who only feeds us baguettes,
Who knew she could be so mean?
We began flying over the pretty skies,
We were thrown into a dungeon,
There were people who only spoke lies,
People with no tongues,
Sandy MacIver dressed as royalty,
Ed Sheeran floating,
Here comes the Ginger Queen,
A crown in her hand, gloating,
I woke, guaranteed it was a dream,
Next to me was the Ginger Queen's crown!

Jazlyn Lee (10)
St Paul's CE Junior School, Barrow-In-Furness

Hyper Hyro The Hippo

Hyper Hyro the hippo and I, travelled across the globe,
Sweat dripped off my head and down my earlobe.
The ice-cold water refreshed in a flash,
Me and Hyro were fighting over a single splash.
Italian pizza and pasta,
England's people bowing down to their master.
I stopped at the shop to get some sweets,
We were never coming to Turkey again as it smelt like feet.

Greece was as hot as the sun,
We went to Spain to visit Hyro's dad and stepmum.
The night we got to Portugal,
All the restaurants there were full.
Arriving in France, we stood in line,
Getting baguettes, croissants, some cheese and wine.
Midnight-blue waters of Antarctica glistened in my eyes,
When having fun; time really flies.
Across the world, Hyro and me have been,
Now it's time to wake up from this wonderful dream.

Evan Coburn (11)
St Paul's CE Junior School, Barrow-In-Furness

Astronaut Footballer

Nothing has prepared me for this amazing land.
Quickly, I run towards it, as nervous as ever.
As I look around, I am shocked that aliens are playing football.
Why am I here? I glance and there are lots of astronauts.
As I step on the football pitch, they ask me to play.
Astronauts vs aliens, who will win?
Powerfully, the ball gets kicked up in the air.
Slowly, it comes back down; I jump and header it up.
Rapidly, the aliens claim the ball again and they score.
My teammate kicks the ball to me, I curl it and score.
There are only two minutes left of the game.
I get the ball, kick it in the top corner; I score in the last minute!
I run over to my teammates to celebrate.
My eyes are shining gold with happiness.
Suddenly, I open my eyes and wake up.
Then I realise it was all just a magical dream.

Lucas Brennan (10)
St Paul's CE Junior School, Barrow-In-Furness

The Blue Cat

I wake up but I'm not in my room,
I see my room, possessions are all around me,
I get up, shoeless.
I realise I'm standing in snowfall,
But the snow is emerald-green,
Ahead of me I see a cerulean cat,
On his head there is a mushroom hat.
Next day, I wake up but I'm not in my room.
Cautiously, I walk a few steps,
My feet as cold as ice,
The midnight-blue feline tells me to sit on his cheese,
I get on, as I was told, and it starts to rise.
It glides at unbelievable speeds,
I meet the moon and it's made out of shining cheese,
I go on an adventure around the electric-yellow planet,
The stars watch us as we fly around,
Then I fall off the cheese.
Fortunately, I wake up before I hit the ground,
But when I wake up, I'm in my room, and it's time for school.

Ameena Miah (11)
St Paul's CE Junior School, Barrow-In-Furness

The Beast Of The Maze

Entering the haunted house, looking for the children,
Didn't know what horrors awaited me,
Thought that if I had friends beside me I'd be alright,
Little did I know there was no real exit,
We entered a room with no sense of danger,
Now we regretted searching,
Hearing a creak, we looked back,
The door closed on us, leaving us deserted,
We glanced behind and what we saw was horrifying,
A tall eerie clown looking down at us creepily,
We sprinted and turned,
In a labyrinth that had no exit,
The beast chasing us with a trail of blood,
Eyes shining and mouth open,
Cables started flying out of his hands,
Seizing my friends suddenly,
One, two, three!
All my friends were gone,
I thought about giving in,
Crash!
The trash compactor had swallowed him whole.

Xander Rayney (10)
St Paul's CE Junior School, Barrow-In-Furness

Dream Poetry

I am walking through the frosty field with Bob.
I see a flying bench speaking from the sky, how random!
My feet are cold, frosty and wet.
It has just begun to rain.
Could this day get any worse?
The bench's wings sound like scrunching paper.
"Look behind you," it cries in a deep, scary voice.
"Arghh! Where is my friend?"
My friend is missing; where has she gone?
Has the bench taken her to a bad place or
A really good place?
Wait! Where has her dog gone?
"Where has her dog gone?"
"Your friend is safe with me, ha ha!" says a mysterious voice.
The fluffy, comfortable cushions look inviting.
A ladder tells me to climb.
Is it trying to trick me?
Will I find my friend?
Or will I get captured?
Who knows what will happen?

Oscar Rowland (10)
St Paul's CE Junior School, Barrow-In-Furness

Midnight

Standing outside,
On a cold winter night.
The snow is going on a ride,
It is windy enough to fly a kite.
Clouds like cotton,
Lunar surface of cheese.
I'm as cold as ice,
In this wintry breeze!
Zoo animals appear from nowhere,
All of them dancing and twirling.
Flying pigs, dogs, butterflies and a giraffe,
A caterpillar slowly unfurling.
I sit on the green grass looking up,
It's a pigeon sat on the moon!
He waves at me and gives me a smile,
I wonder what's coming soon?
I get a shock, when I relive my dream.
Under covers, cosy as can be.
Is it real? Did I really see that?
Or was it just me being me?

Georgia Royle (11)
St Paul's CE Junior School, Barrow-In-Furness

The Alien Octopus

Trees tumbling down,
Wind blowing me backwards.
An unrecognisable creature flies out of the water,
Frightening me out of my wits!
My best friend is as cold as ice,
Getting drenched by the creature.
The unknown predator uses its power,
Boom!
The alien octopus strikes with its rocky throw,
The tentacled creature captures my friend.
How do I save him?
This is as scary as a nightmare.
I dodge the watery splash from the mysterious beast,
My friend gathers rocks
While I start throwing pebbles at the monster.
My friend catapults a rock right into its mouth,
Then it disintegrates into the Earth.

Noah Olliver (11)
St Paul's CE Junior School, Barrow-In-Furness

A Fantasy Battle Of Good And Evil

Normal fairies, normal village,
Everything was ordinary,
Not a single problem,
As the fantasy forest surrounded me.

Mushroom flowers,
Trees and my people,
Gather every May,
Towards the wishing tree,
To make the perfect day,
An open portal appeared in the tree,
An evil witch emerged.

The fairies were shaken,
Lots of things ruined,
But everything she took,
The pixies knew what to do,
They worked together,
As what they had to do the most,
Was make sure they got their power.

The witch fought well, the pixies fought better,
The witch was defeated by the power of together.

Hallie Thomas (11)
St Paul's CE Junior School, Barrow-In-Furness

Bell Scores

All the lionesses are depending on me,
Especially Phoebe and my mum.
I start up-front with Georgia Stanway on my right and Phoebe on my left.
I know this is a big game.
The game starts. I pass it to Phoebe.
I get the ball, I go around the players.
With the ball, I try to shoot but I miss.
Kelly takes the corner. Phoebe headers it. Score!
Everyone is cheering and clapping.
I run back and the game starts again.
I get the ball, I pass it to Kelly,
Kelly passes it back.
I shoulder-barge the defenders and I get through.
I score top bins!
I feel the joy and look at my mum,
Her smile is the best reward!

Hollie Bell (10)
St Paul's CE Junior School, Barrow-In-Furness

The Silly Queen

I'm in my dream,
Fallen through a talking fountain,
I can see sparkling trees,
Different types of leaves,
There are eye-gazing murals upon the ground.
In an eagerly enchanted wood,
I've just seen the queen as I am skipping through the woods,
She's wearing a beautiful sky-blue dress that looks amazing,
The Silly Queen is a great leader,
She has a bright red crown,
Her headdress is blinding me with its brightness!
We've now come to an aggressive monster howling,
But the Silly Queen has got out her sword...
I wake up from my dream!

Scarlett Parkinson (11)
St Paul's CE Junior School, Barrow-In-Furness

Circus Day Out

It is time to go to the circus,
What will I do there?
Will I make it out alive?
Am I even going to go?
What if I get a surprise,
I hope not!
I've found a robot on stage,
I'm here alone, it can't be the end,
As I wander on the stage, I hear the robot cry,
Its wail sounding like a child,
Eyes glowing red like it's part of something evil,
It looks me dead in the eyes; I can't move,
What will it do to me?
Its voice is cracking,
It is glitching,
I need help,
I wake up quickly, I was only dreaming.

Lilly Keogh (10)
St Paul's CE Junior School, Barrow-In-Furness

The Fairy Dance

In my dreams,
Imps watch the fairy twirl,
Brownies spot the gnome swirl.
On the bouncy toadstool,
They dance the fairy dance.
Thousands of eyes stare,
Nobody could g are.
All watch the sprites,
Whirling round the mushroom.
Her wings flap,
Her feet slap,
Under the emerald awning.
They spiral as one,
Together they eat snacks,
Joyfully they play catch,
Not a single fault
In the pixie village.
Many fairy friends join them,
Trees sway along with the elves,
The dance lasts for hours.

Penny Brough (10)
St Paul's CE Junior School, Barrow-In-Furness

The Seagull In A Suit

On a normal, windy, winter evening,
Freezing air brushed against my fingertips.
As cold as ice,
I heard a squawking noise.
A seagull on a bin,
Screeching and shrieking at anyone who looked at it.
Not like any other seagull,
This one had a suit and a cane.
He did a fancy twirl and dance,
Sticking out his wing as if I should shake.
I was at a loss for words,
The bird was certainly a unique one.
He started talking to me and proposed a deal,
I would have to get him food and clothes.
In return, I would get a reward,
I realised this was going to be an interesting dream.

Jess Renshaw (10)
St Paul's CE Junior School, Barrow-In-Furness

Flying Fish And The Squid

A beautiful flying fish,
Playing the amazing sport football,
With a flying squid,
It's the squid versus the fish,
I can see the pond,
Hear the fans cheering,
Me and my friends go fishing,
When I see the game begin,
I enter the water with my friends,
They disappear, they prank me,
It's starting to rain,
We rush to the stands,
We observe the squid dancing,
Cheering on their football team,
The fish scores!
He begins to disappear,
The dream is over,
Who will score tomorrow?

Carter Deakin (10)
St Paul's CE Junior School, Barrow-In-Furness

The Unicorn And The World Of Dream Creatures

In my dreams every night,
I see a magical sight,
A colourful unicorn rainbow too,
Around me I see
The beautiful world of dream creatures.
I feel excited,
The unicorn picks me up,
What is it doing?
It starts running,
Looking down I see
The ground below me.
Get covered by a magical glow of colour,
A rainbow!
I look up and see the glowing moon,
Shining in the mystical night sky,
I hear my name,
It's time to wake.
See you tomorrow in my dreams.

Elicia Thompson (10)
St Paul's CE Junior School, Barrow-In-Furness

The Septadragon

I see the salty sea,
Feel the soft sand on my cold toes,
Wind is loud in my ears,
As I spot the palm trees and coconuts on the island ahead,
Suddenly!
The island ascends skywards,
It's a septadragon!
Running for the hills,
Tripping over logs,
It senses me and begins its attack.
Too weak to run,
I see a piece of metal, grab it to me.
It's coming fast,
I leap and whack it hard,
I'm in its labyrinth-like mouth!
My nightmare has begun...

Zebulon Morrison (10)
St Paul's CE Junior School, Barrow-In-Furness

A Spider And A Giraffe

A beautiful spider
Wearing sparkly heels
A scarlet-red dress
Dancing on Strictly
One twirl here
One twirl there
Here she goes
Going in for the somersault
She lands it!
She did it!
The crowd is amazed
They all start cheering
A giraffe in a tuxedo
Wearing some loafers
Comes onto the stage
For a cheeky little dance
Two legs are better than eight!
He twirls
He shimmies
The judges choose... and it's Giraffe!

Georgia-Mae Frazer (11)
St Paul's CE Junior School, Barrow-In-Furness

Puffball And The Amazing Camera

I grab my balloons,
Floating on high,
I see a sign that says puffball,
A panda with big bushy ears,
His hand holds a camera,
He lives in the clouds above,
This shows me all his pictures,
His bushy fur is as soft as candyfloss,
But don't be fooled,
Puff can become a monster!
I haven't made him angry yet,
Let's hope that stays the same,
Happy Puff doesn't make a fuss,
I don't want my dream to become a nightmare!

Rosie Peel (10)
St Paul's CE Junior School, Barrow-In-Furness

Dream Poem

I saw a dragon in the clouds,
I could see the sky-blue and fire-red,
It smelt like a dustbin.
My friends and I went to fight it,
It was as tough as a tiger,
Had fire-booster on it,
Used its tail as a whip.
I felt scared, worried and anxious,
Thrash! Crash! Bang!
Sword and dragon hide clashing,
Back and forth, back and forth,
Who would win the fight?
You guessed it. I would,
Dream victory once again.

Hadley Hill (10)
St Paul's CE Junior School, Barrow-In-Furness

The Magic Of Imagination

In a world of dreams, and make-believe,
Where anything is possible, you'll perceive,
Unicorns prancing in fields so green,
And talking animals, a magical scene.

With a sprinkle of stardust, let your mind soar,
To places unseen, where adventures galore,
Fly with fairies, swim with mermaids too,
The magic of imagination, all for you.

So close your eyes, let your thoughts take flight,
Create a world that's filled with delight,
In your imagination the possibilities are vast,
Where dreams come alive and memories are cast.

M aybe it's a real great thing.
A n imagination thing.
G reat ideas for this.
I magination land for a dream.
C reative dream for a normal brain.

Favour Ndikum (8)
Warren Farm Primary School, Kingstanding

The Enchanted Lake

If you venture deep into Tail Twister Wood,
They dance by the buttercups where the tree wisest stood,
It whispers and sways before showing you,
The opening to a world where everything is true.

Then go a little further,
And be careful not to wake,
The sleeping forest giants,
But now you're at the Enchanted Lake.

With pixies flying overhead,
And magical dancing flowers,
Be careful of the fairy dust,
And its amazing powers!

The ripples on the water,
Sparkle in the sun,
It's turquoise like gleaming diamonds,
A treat for anyone!

Trees of every colour stand,
Pink, orange and green,
And the luscious grass that surrounds,
Is the most delightful thing you've ever seen.

So next time you are in Tail Twister Woods,
Please dance by the buttercups where the wisest tree stood,
Watch it whisper and sway before showing you,
The magical world where everything is true!

Please go a little further,
Just be careful not to wake,
The sleeping forest giants,
But then you'll be at the Enchanted Lake.

Evie Gouldingay (10)

Warren Farm Primary School, Kingstanding

Pirate Boy

Across the sea,
Where no one will be,
On a wonderful island,
A little boy in the sand,
See a pirate,
Wearing violet,
The pirate sees the boy,
While he's playing with a toy,
He comes over,
With his parrot called Rover,
Puts the boy to sleep,
Crowded with sheep,
Carries the boy over to his base,
The boy wakes up and tries to tie his lace,
The pirate has a potion,
Although no smellies, or lotion,
He gives it to the boy,
"Here drink this,"
Doesn't want to give a kiss.
The boy drinks it,
He gives out a spit,
"Aarrrh! Me maties,"
Forgetting the evil god, Hades,

"Yes, he's a pirate," the pirate says,
The mission not even taking him days,
The pirate's really happy.
The boy wakes up hearing cries from
A baby with a dirty nappy.

Harry Davies (8)
Warren Farm Primary School, Kingstanding

The Magical Forest

I walked through a magical forest,
I saw glowing butterflies.
Ancient trees, with branches that soar,
Hold secrets of dreams from days of yore.

In this realm where reality grows,
A dreamscape forest, where wishes ascend.
Mystical creatures, silent and wise,
Dwell among the shadows with starlit eyes.

Through the glade, where soft breezes hum,
Dreams take flight, a symphony of the drum.
Golden hues of an ethereal dawn,
Paint the skies where dreams are drawn.

Each step echoes in the enchanted air,
In this forest, where dreams declare.
Fairies dance in a shimmering trance,
As moonbeams weave a dreamscape dance.

Under the canopy where the stars align,
A magical forest, where dreams entwine.

Maison Crofts (10)
Warren Farm Primary School, Kingstanding

My Dream Job

I want to be a singer and a designer,
Sometimes I think about being a mountain climber,
I want to be an actress and in the Olympics,
Maybe a gymnast when I can do the splits,
I want to be a doctor, but I couldn't be,
I'd be far too scared to see blood everywhere,
There are so many jobs that I want to do,
One thing's for sure, it's going to be hard to choose,
I've got to pick, quick, there's no time to lose,
Whatever shall I be? Whatever shall I do?
I see the kids around me, with their lives planned out,
While I'm sitting here, finding it hard to figure out,
These kids have known it all since they were babies,
Only in diapers, they knew their course for university!

Thiciane Alynne Junqueira De Andrade (9)
Warren Farm Primary School, Kingstanding

Lola And The Enchanted Forest

Once upon a dream,
There was a stream,
In an enchanted forest,
Where there was a bunch of flowers,
Meanwhile, a girl called Lola was running from her friends,
She spotted a magical gate,
Inside she saw spiders and clowns.
Lola kept walking and then entered a portal.
Lola was soon in a magical place.
She saw fairies, dinosaurs dragons and so on,
Twelve princesses led her to a castle,
She met the king, who was her long-lost father.
Her mother came and told her everything.
Lola was actually a princess.
Her father was the king and her mother was the queen.
They wanted her to have a normal life.
After that, they lived happily ever after.

Hope Matangwe (9)
Warren Farm Primary School, Kingstanding

The Famous Flying Dancer

The famous flying dancer leaping through the air,
Twisting, twirling, flying without a care.
Skipping through the clouds, swirling all around,
Annabel, the flying dancer, flounces for the town.

All the people are watching her with *oohs*, *wows* and *ahhs*,
Twirling, swirling in the sky, she's a dancing shooting star.

Look at her go, look at her grace, look at the smile upon her face.

She flies through the sky like a bird in the blue,
She hears the sound of a *cock-a-doodle-do*.

She opens her eyes to the sun's bright gleam.
To Annabel's surprise, it was just a joyous dream.

Hollie Treharne (9)
Warren Farm Primary School, Kingstanding

Dragon Dreams!

I rode on a dragon,
Far across the sky,
Where a gust of wind,
Blew right into my eyes.

I let go of the dragon,
Then suddenly fell off,
I landed on a cloud,
The dragon shouted, "Mazel tov!"

I looked up to the dragon,
Feeling so confused,
Then a TV appeared,
To share some breaking news...

It's going to rain cupcakes,
So shout hip hip hooray,
The dragon came with a box,
Saying happy birthday.

I was so excited,
I went to give him a hug,
But then I kept falling,
And woke up on my bedroom rug.

Maiya Ceesay (9)
Warren Farm Primary School, Kingstanding

Lost With Cameron

Cameron midst the wood's shadows play,
Nature's challenge in the light of day.
Through thicket a winding trail,
Whispers beckon, like a hidden tale.
Lost with Cameron in the emerald-green,
Nature's mystery, a world unseen.
Under canopy where sunlight wanes,
Cameron wanders, breaking nature's chains.
A symphony of leaves rustle and hum,
In the heart of the forest his senses become.
Each step a question, each path a choice,
Lost with Cameron, he finds his voice.
The journey unfolds a tapestry of green,
Lost with Cameron, a poem yet unseen.

Abdullateef Ayantola (9)
Warren Farm Primary School, Kingstanding

My Dreams

In my dreams at night,
Sometimes I get a fright,
Other nights, I meet a fairy,
Or I learn how to bake cakes light and airy,
I sometimes play guitar,
Or I'm sitting in my car!
Most times, I'm amazingly happy,
And meet a crocodile who is quite snappy,
I have a unicorn called Moonbeam,
Who's not as quiet as she seems,
As well as my fairy pal, Daisy,
Who's actually quite lazy,
These are my different dreams,
I love them as much as my family.

Olivia Nottingham (9)
Warren Farm Primary School, Kingstanding

Unicorn Rescue

Unicorns are running down the street
How can this be if I'm meant to be asleep?
With a run and a jump, they fly into the sky
So fast I couldn't even say goodbye.

Walking in the dark,
Ahead I see the park
A trapped unicorn I see
I need to set him free.

Wrapped in a football net
Cold and alone
I will help, so he can go home.

I pull out my scissors
This is my dream
Let's be quick
So he doesn't get seen.

Lexi Barmer (8)
Warren Farm Primary School, Kingstanding

The Football Dream

Playing football, I would see
Ronaldo, Haaland and Messi
We will win because of me
The team we play for, Inter Miami

The crowd will go wild when I do a trick
It feels amazing, great, fantastic
I win back the ball, the tackle is sick
I feel I will score a big hat-trick

No one could believe what they saw
When I scored thirty goals, then more
Everyone's jaw was on the floor
Then I won the Golden Boot and the Ballon d'Or.

Harley Bree (8)
Warren Farm Primary School, Kingstanding

The Other World

I can see villains running wild.
Can I save the city?
I am only a child,
But with my powers,
I can stop anything that devours.
Now there's dragons going left and right,
Giving everyone a fright,
Then I realise I'm in the land,
Where the evil wizard makes his plans.
In the blink of an eye, the sorcerer comes and whispers,
"Hi,"
And I shout, "Off with your head!"
But find out I'm safe in bed.

Bobby Nottingham (9)
Warren Farm Primary School, Kingstanding

My Dreams

Once I had a dream,
I was flying in the air,
And magically I saw a bear.

Once I had a dream,
I was singing with the fairies,
And they gave me some delicious berries.

Once I had a dream,
I was jumping with the frogs,
And then I got hit by a log,

Once I had a dream,
I was riding a dragon,
And it was pulling a nice pink wagon.

Until,
I woke up and saw the time,
It was 9:29!

YaXin Wang (10)
Warren Farm Primary School, Kingstanding

Bunny-Fairies

Bad fairies put me to sleep,
Bunnies all over me in my dream,
So far away, I can't think.
Please help me, good fairies,
To escape this dream.

Mountains, fossils, bunnies everywhere,
In my dream, snowflakes on top of Buttercup Mountain
In Canada, I can see.
Let me wake up from this dreadful dream,
As my eyes flicker open,
I can see my mum,
But now I'm safe and sound!

Amelia Bravington-Bryant (8)
Warren Farm Primary School, Kingstanding

Dreams

D reams are images and symbols that appear in your mind.
R emembering all the good things that happen and can take you to a special place.
E ntering all of the wonderful places that you believe are magical.
A way we go into the dream world with all our loved ones with us.
M irroring memories that can last a lifetime.
S weet dreams without nightmares are the best.

Harry Martin (7)
Warren Farm Primary School, Kingstanding

A Boy Who Is Sleeping

In a deep slumber,
Dreaming of calling birds singing,
A melodic musical number,
With enormous bells ringing,
Dreams are a place of fun,
With unicorns roaming and phoenixes flying,
All around the sun,
Melodies being vocalised by multicoloured birds,
Remember, this is all imagination,
And dragons fly above fields in herds,
These ferocious beasts are a huge attraction.

Emmanuel Sambayi (9)
Warren Farm Primary School, Kingstanding

African Royalty

Beneath the African shining sun so bright
Kings and queens stand tall and right
In fields where lions softly roam
They lead with kindness, hearts like home
With smiles wide and hands that guide
They keep their people safe inside
In Africa's heart, their stories glow
Like rivers deep they always grow.

Modesireoluwa Soyannwo
Warren Farm Primary School, Kingstanding

Imagine Having Superpowers

Imagine having superpowers and being able to fly,
Imagine running really fast and levitating through the sky,
I'm getting mixed emotions,
I think I just drank a bunch of potions,
I'm running with The Flash,
I can finally dash,
My dream has come to an end,
I'm sad that it was all pretend.

Cameron Orbell (9)
Warren Farm Primary School, Kingstanding

Sunderland Star

Sunderland, Sunderland,
Brightest star.
Lots of goals in the net!

Sunderland have Jobe and Clarke.
Sunderland better be in the Prem!

They should be in the Prem
Because they are better than Aston Villa,
Because they can't score properly.

Arlo Martin (7)
Warren Farm Primary School, Kingstanding

The Power Of A Dream

The power of a dream
Can make you seem different than usual.
The power of a dream.

You can be running but not moving,
In another dream, grooving.
Silence in your bedroom,
But a scream in your dream.
The power of a dream.

Destiny Clayton (10)
Warren Farm Primary School, Kingstanding

Moon Jump

While I'm in bed,
Something scary happened in my head.
Someone asked me, "Truth or dare?"
Nothing happened but I said, "Dare."
They dared me to jump to the moon from a faraway place,
I shrugged my shoulders and we were face-to-face.
I took a giant run backwards and soon got hurt,
I fell over and asked, "Are you sure this is going to work?"
He said, "Yes, yes, yes."
But I said, "No, you're such a pest."
I ran backwards to North America and took a big jump,
I closed my eyes, "I'm sure I'm going to bump!"
When I opened my eyes, I could not believe it,
I had jumped from North America to a moon-pit.
I saw planets, stars and friendly aliens too,
"I better not tread in some alien poo!"
When I jumped back to the darer,
I told him, "I did it!" but I was filled with terror.
I opened my eyes and it was 7 o'clock,
So I ran to my mummy's room and told her what happened.

She said, "It must have been a shock."
I whispered, *"It was just a dream."*
Mum said, "Oh the moon jump sounds so extreme!"

Luke Pateman (7)
Whirley Primary School, Macclesfield

The Magical Unicorn

M ighty unicorns travelling across the land,
A ggressively galloping to a portal,
G rasping onto the portal, they fall inside.
I nside the portal, they see another dimension,
C autiously they help another unicorn,
A s they get out the unicorn greets them,
L oudly they stomp away.

U sually, they spy on other unicorns,
N ow they have to protect their coins from the unicorn thief,
I f they don't go quietly they will wake him up.
C an they make it to Ice Cream Land?
O nce they get through to rescue Mum and Dad from the dungeon,
R aspberry Ripple River was in front of the dungeon, how could they help their parents?
N ow they had to give all their coins to the unicorn king.

Bobby Villers (8)
Whirley Primary School, Macclesfield

Why Is This Happening?

One day, me and my dad decided to go to a football match.
As we got into the stadium it was already 1-0 to City because we were late.

At half-time, it was 5-0 to Manchester City,
Suddenly I got really tired,
I desperately wanted to watch the game but I was already asleep before I could even think.

A gust of wind blew across my face,
I opened my eyes and jumped in shock,
No one was there,
I rubbed my eyes and nothing changed,
My instant thought was to run onto the pitch to have some fun!

I went to sit on all the sub benches,
And finally Pep's seat,
A few minutes later I knew this was not a joke.
My conscience came back into play,
I saw everyone chanting,
And myself getting dragged out of the stadium by security!

Lucas Scott (11)
Whirley Primary School, Macclesfield

Trapped In A Time Loop

I'm in a room.
It's pitch-black, apart from the small glow
Of a melting candle.
I look around, and a shiver crawls down my spine,
As it's cold and spooky.
I look at the time. 12am.
I stand there for a while,
Waiting for it to turn 12:01am,
But it never happens.
What's going on? Am I stuck in a loop?
I close my eyes, hoping this is just a nightmare.
I feel a cold breeze as my heart starts to thump.
I peek through my eyelids only to see
That nothing has changed,
Apart from the doll sitting on the shelf.
It seems like its eyes have moved
And I swear its hand was on its chest before.
I rub my eyes, hoping that this really is just a nightmare,
But nothing happens.
Am I stuck here?

Lilliana Millward (10)
Whirley Primary School, Macclesfield

Deep In The Woods

D arkness surrounds me as I fall asleep
E ver closer to the crooked old cabin I creep
E xcited and anxious I look through the window
P otions like the shelves in colours of the rainbow

I n through the open door, I sneak into the room
N ot noticing the evil witch behind me in the gloom.

T oo late!
H ypnotised so I don't remember or see
E yeballs in the bubbling cauldron staring up at me.

W ishing I'd not wandered deep into the wood
O pening the cabin door was certainly not good
O nwards I stumble until
D awn begins to break then
S uddenly I sit up and I'm wide awake.

Esme Cope (10)
Whirley Primary School, Macclesfield

A Million Dreams

Every night, my dreams take flight, colours fill my head,
Sometimes yellow, sometimes blue, also red,
All different shapes and sizes,
Moonbeam bright as black as the midnight sky,
Going down holes as pink as ever,
Lands of red, plains of blue,
Vibrant purple to the rose coloured pink,
Dots of moonlight white that float into a circle of red,
Moving things of majestic indigo,
A non-frightening land of peace and love,
Lovely patterns of blue and red,
Emerald-green to the nightshade of violet,
Sunshine-yellow to calming sapphire,
Pink circles surrounding a midnight-black land,
After that I may be woken,
But maybe still in a fascinating dream.

Amara Lamptey-Spencer (7)
Whirley Primary School, Macclesfield

A Dream

A dream is something special,
It's fun and fantastic.
Close your eyes, count to three
And you'll be teleported to a world of your own.
Your dream might be adventurous or mythical and many more
And if you dream it hard enough it might become real.
So now think of what you want to do,
Or you could have a dream or two.
You'll never regret it,
You'll have so much fun,
If you think I'm lying well think again.
Without dreams you wouldn't be living in a world like this
Because this world all started with a dream,
So if you're feeling sad just take a minute to dream,
You'll feel much better, just wait and see.

Holly Delaney (9)
Whirley Primary School, Macclesfield

The Contact Rugby Dream

C ontact rugby is so good,
O nly the tough, like playing in the mud,
N ot many people like playing in the rain,
T hey find it a real pain,
A lthough I'm only eight and this is just a dream,
C an't wait until I'm old enough to play contact with my team,
T errific tales have come back from others,

R unning past everyone, dodging tackles, but not for the mothers,
U nfortunately, sometimes you do get hurt,
G ot to put their hands over their faces and also face a muddy shirt,
B all gets carried over the line,
Y ou cheer and say, "That try is mine!"

Max Handley (8)
Whirley Primary School, Macclesfield

A Dream Away

Fading away,
My story is finished,
They're close to the final chapter.
The ink is running out,
The pen is off.

The pages are disappearing,
Where has the time gone?
I don't know, I don't know.

Cold shivers are running down my spine.
My heart skips a beat.
Is this a happy ending?
I don't know, I don't know.

Is it possible, I'm like Sleeping Beauty?
But my prince never came.
My heart has been poisoned
From the prick of a wheel.
Where did the time go?
I don't know, I don't know.

My hair, as long as a tower,
I know I will find my happy ending!

Isabelle Hibberts (11)
Whirley Primary School, Macclesfield

The Pirate Adventure

Every night, I hope and dream,
Now let me show you where I've been,
It began in the sea,
Swimming as happy as can be,
Swimming there was me and Beth,
Going so fast, we were out of breath,
In the distance, we could see,
A pirate ship coming towards me,
A pirate crew welcomed us aboard,
And we bowed to the big pirate lord,
They made it seem like we were one of their own,
A huge welcome party was thrown.
They gave us some pirate gear,
For us to stay with them all year,
With a stretch and a yawn I opened my eyes,
And it was dawn,
My next pirate adventure awaits,
For when I go to bed at eight.

Ava McClelland (8)
Whirley Primary School, Macclesfield

Snakes And Ladders Gone Wrong

I closed my eyes...
A colourful arcade appeared in front of me.
Stepping through the door, the flashing neon lights made me want to explore.
My favourite game of Snakes and Ladders.
I pressed the start button and suddenly I was lifted off my feet.
The game sucked me in and I came face-to-face with a terrifyingly, ferocious snake!
Trembling with fear, I tiptoed over to the nearest ladder.
I carefully climbed, looking for my escape.
It seemed like forever but finally I could see the top!
My eyes were opening and I could feel my comfy bed underneath me.
"Morning Mum. Oh, it was just a dream!"

Olive McGillivray (8)
Whirley Primary School, Macclesfield

The Secret Land Of Monsters

In my dream, I have a land,
And I'm accompanied by a band,
They're small furry and insane,
These idiot crazy creatures, they're a real big pain.
I see a horned, vicious monster in the dusty cave,
His head is bald, he had to shave.
These monsters are the newest craze,
Then an oozy monster stepped out the lake,
The creepy, scary vibes gave me an ache,
It is an eyeball watching me,
This creepy stare is always free.
A bulgy crab crawls from the floor,
Its crabby pincers click for more,
And suddenly my vision goes,
And now my dream is literally over!

Jacob Eaton (9)
Whirley Primary School, Macclesfield

Pirates Of The Caribbean: The Stranded Captain!

My boat was rapidly sinking,
My brain hastily was thinking,
I washed up at a port,
No clue where I was of any sort.
There was no one around,
But suddenly I found,
The golden treasure,
And that was a pleasure.
Suddenly, a monster,
A scary hairy whopper,
From out of the deep dark,
Much bigger than a shark,
As the sweat dripped down my skin,
The air was cold and thin,
I quickly sprinted away,
It took me about a day.
I ran out of the creature's sight,
Hoping not to fight.
Now with my gold,
I stood tall and bold.

Arthur Gerrard (8)
Whirley Primary School, Macclesfield

Macc Juniors

It was a Saturday afternoon,
I couldn't see the moon.
Macc Juniors vs Juno Jaguars,
The most competitive game of the year.

I drank and drank,
I felt like I'd robbed a bank.
I could see my ultimate dream,
There was a lucky twist in the team.

The magic was amazing, I wanted it to last
I got a free kick and my foot went *blast!*
A bicycle-kick
Their goalie was sick
Wembley was the best day
The whole crowd went hip hip hooray.

Macc Juniors won the title and lifted the trophy,
What a day!

Charlie Macey (8)
Whirley Primary School, Macclesfield

A Walk I Won't Forget

Wandering through the forest – just my mum and me,
When I catch a glimpse of something,
Behind a big oak tree,
I stare and squint and rub my eyes,
Thinking, *what could this be?*
When suddenly, I realise
It's a little wallaby!

It's brown and fluffy, soft and cute,
With big, long, pointy ears,
I scoop him up and hold him tight,
In case he disappears,
I think I'll call him Freddie,
He's my super bouncy pet,
I'll take him home and snuggle up with him,
This is a walk I won't forget!

Will Heywood (9)
Whirley Primary School, Macclesfield

The Wedding

There was a unicorn called Ted,
Who was fast asleep in his bed,
He was madly in love with a fairy,
And everyone knew it was Mary.

They lived in a beautiful wood,
Where nearly all the people were good,
Ted got on a knee near a sparkling stream,
And his question made Mary's smile gleam.

Before the wedding I started to bake,
The most wonderful sprinkle cake,
We put the cake in a really nice box,
Which sneakily got taken by Fox.

My jokes in a speech caused laughter,
And they all lived happily ever after.

Evie Ashcroft (7)
Whirley Primary School, Macclesfield

Untitled

F ootball is the best hobby,
O wen used to be a legend for Liverpool,
O ne hundred and fifty-eight goals Owen scored,
T rent is a brilliant defender for Liverpool,
B ernardo Silva is a fantastic midfielder for Man City,
A lexis MacAlliser is a really good midfielder for Liverpool,
L istening to managers to help them train,
L osing matches helps us to learn from our mistakes,
E gypt is one of the best teams for the World Cup,
R eal Madrid has the best team in Spain.

Flynn Simister (8)
Whirley Primary School, Macclesfield

Pedal To The Cardboard: My F1 Journey!

F ast around the track, my cardboard racer speeds.
O ver the hills and through the valleys, fulfilling my needs.
R oaring engines in dreams, where I lead the pack.
M y F1 car of cardboard, on the imaginary track.
U nder the stars, racing with glee.
L aps of victory, as fast as can be.
A head of the rest, in my own Grand Prix.

O nly the wind for company, wild and free.
N ight-time adventures, where I take the throne.
E very turn a story, in a league of my own.

Max Joseph Brown (10)
Whirley Primary School, Macclesfield

A Sky Dream

On a twilight night,
When the silver moon shines bright,
Past some silly clowns,
And above the fluffy clouds.
Lots of fairies and unicorns fly free,
And loads of other wonderful things to see.
I find myself on a unicorn with my cousin Bloom,
We meet fairies as we zoom.
The fairies give us magic food,
It makes me feel in a good mood.
We climb an orange and yellow tree,
I hang off a branch with glee.
Suddenly I'm falling, oh no, will I bang my head?
Luckily, I have a soft landing in my bed.

Bella Heyes (8)
Whirley Primary School, Macclesfield

The Space Adventure

I'm in the rocket on my way to space,
Three, two, one, blast-off! This is ace!
I look around and I can see,
A shooting star flying over me.
When I look closer, aliens are waving,
Are they waving or do they need saving?
We need this rocket to go really fast,
I push the button, we are off with a blast.
It's dark in space and I miss home,
I want to go back, my dog is alone.
We land back on Earth with a crash and a bang,
"Welcome home, Captain Roy," the crowd cheered and sang.

Rory Owen (7)
Whirley Primary School, Macclesfield

Gaming Dream

G aming on my Xbox
A lways as quick as a fox
M y controller blue like the sea
I magining me versus a Minecraft zombie
N ow we're in a fight
G oing fist to fist, victory is in sight

D amage! I hit him with a diamond sword
R eally close to getting the Monster Hunter award
E nding the fight I feel great
A nd I'm hopping around with my mate
M y dream's now come to an end, and morning is just around the bend.

Oliver Pateman (10)
Whirley Primary School, Macclesfield

Future Dreams

My eyes close tight but I can still see clearly.
A young woman with hazel-brown hair is caring so dearly.
She talks to an unfamiliar figure,
The panic on their face grows bigger,
Confidently she enters a room, a pet in her arms,
She works on the pet and puts her head on their heart but does no harm.
Fireflies dance around her head,
"And, all done," she says.
She turns and looks at me,
Can she see?
Who is she? I wonder...
Oh, it's just future me!

Nola Campbell (10)
Whirley Primary School, Macclesfield

Blade Quest

A young Japanese man was fighting for a magical sword,
He was fighting for his Lord.
And the glass shattered around the board.

As he faced the guardians of the blade,
A shiver ran down his spine but his fear did fade.

He summoned the gods and cast a spell.
And all around the guardians fell.

He stepped forward to claim his magic knife,
The weapon shone and glowed with life.

He hopped on his horse and headed West,
Now he had completed his magical quest.

Jasper Bains (10)
Whirley Primary School, Macclesfield

Imagination

I was floating in the air,
M y head was spinning with my hair,
A cat was dancing in the street,
G rinning to look at me our eyes then meet,
I saw a dog hopping around,
N ot the most funny thing I'd found.
A giraffe was wearing goggles and a swimming costume,
T hen went flying down a fast log flume.
I t then made a splash,
O ver a dog doing the monster mash.
N o, it was not real... It was just a dream.

Erin Tench (9)
Whirley Primary School, Macclesfield

Outer Space

The galactic space,
Will be left without a trace,
The dancing stars,
Zoom past flying cars,
I wonder as I speak,
I hope nothing turns bleak,
Hopping from planet to planet,
Magical dust floats down as if from a packet,
Jar after jar illuminates the twinkling night,
With colours galactic bright,
From a galaxy far beyond,
Floating inwards I can feel a bond,
Will my dreams come true?
Or will they be cursed like an everlasting cauldron brew?

Ellie Norbury (10)
Whirley Primary School, Macclesfield

It's Not Her, It's Me

Backstage before the show,
She's ready with her celebrity glow.
Hearing the distant sound of the crowd,
She knows tonight she'll sing loud and proud.
It's time to go to the stage as the clock hits zero,
She will open with 'Anti-Hero'.
Now the crowd go wild,
She stepped into the lights and smiled.

As thoughts go round my mind of Taylor Swift,
I slowly start to drift.
Now I can clearly see
It's not her, it's me!

Eliza Utteridge (8)
Whirley Primary School, Macclesfield

My Dance Dream

My dance dream is to enter the IDTA Dance Theatre Awards,
And do well.
I dream of becoming a tap winner in the future.
I dream of doing many auditions and shows,
Winning awards for ballet, tap, modern, contemporary, jazz, acro and more.

My dance dream is to win the IDTA Awards,
I become a tap winner.
I dream of passing auditions and doing great in shows,
Winning awards for ballet, tap modern contemporary, jazz, acro and more.
My dance dream!

Millie Harrad (10)
Whirley Primary School, Macclesfield

Football!

F ootball is a game of strength and it's an awesome game to play!
O n an awesome sunny day, they try to do their best to win,
O utside a stadium, there are trillions of cars in the parking lot,
T he crowd roars loudly with every goal,
B ut they always say practice makes perfect,
A ttack and trackback,
L osing is normal you just need to win next time,
L eaping for the ball so that you can try and score!

Aiden Choi (8)
Whirley Primary School, Macclesfield

The Teddy Adventure

Last night, whilst I was sleeping, all my teddies came alive,
Flapjack ate bananas and Pudding went for a drive,
Rooney on the chimney pot doing lots of drawing,
Daisy the cow playing football doing lots of scoring,
Fluff Bean putting on ten shoes, getting ready for a walk,
Ruff Ruff, he's my favourite, and he can finally talk,
I wonder what he would say to me now he has a voice,
"I love you, Beth, with all my heart," what a lovely choice.

Beth Shaul (7)
Whirley Primary School, Macclesfield

Possibilities For The Future

P eople in the future,
O ften have advanced technology.
S uper smart AI running the house,
S leek self-driving cars dominate the road,
I nvasion of the robots could be a possibility!
B ut is this how the world should be?
I n reality, all this technology might not be a good thing.
L ost connections,
I nformation overload,
T oo many devices,
Y ou think this is a good idea?

Isaac Cockburn (11)
Whirley Primary School, Macclesfield

Enchanted City

In my dream, I dream about...

M agical cities all around
E nchanted trees on every ground
R ummaging through the bushes and trees
M ermaids waiting in the emerald-blue seas
A tlantis down in the deep blue sea
I ncredible things await me
D azzling animals in the sea
S ea creatures all staring at me.

But now my dream is coming to an end,
So see you soon, my very best friend.

Mia Scragg (10)
Whirley Primary School, Macclesfield

Mystery And The Dragon World

In the middle of the night
In my dream
Deep in the jet-black wood
I was all alone
Suddenly I looked behind a bush
And saw a new world
A dragon world
I hesitated for a moment
And then stepped inside
It was beautiful
I saw flying dragons
Even mini baby dragons
They were so cute
All of a sudden
I looked behind me
And then glanced back again
And the world had gone
Was it a dream
Or was it real?

Matilda Naughton (8)
Whirley Primary School, Macclesfield

The Unicorn

M aisie loves flying with her soft wings,
A nd she loves apples and tasty things,
G reen like grass she loves,
I n fact, she likes flying with powers,
C hasing cats, she absolutely hates.

W ind she flies through with her best mates,
I ce she can definitely not walk on,
N icely, she flew to be gone,
G oing along with her friend, Fairy,
S o it doesn't feel that scary.

Emily Stewart (8)
Whirley Primary School, Macclesfield

Once Upon A Dream

As I snuggle under my covers,
I close my eyes,
What will I discover?
I can see the sun lighting up in the sky,
As I start my journey,
And begin to fly

I see Mickey and Minnie
With grins so wide,
Guiding my dream on a magical ride,
Donald and Daisy walking with cheer and delight,
My dream continues,
In this magical night,
The Disney characters snuggled me up in my cosy covers,
Knowing what I discovered!

Molly Macey (11)
Whirley Primary School, Macclesfield

Daydream

D rifting through clear, cloudy skies
A dventure! We could see it with our eyes
"**Y** ippee! Disneyland!" I shouted with joy.
D isneyland characters everywhere, fun for every girl and boy
R ides spread laughter around the place
E very firework banged and glimmered on my face
A s the fireworks ended, I shivered to my bones
M y fun day was over, but I really didn't want to go home.

Lola Rowson (8)
Whirley Primary School, Macclesfield

The Croaky Frog

In my dreams every night,
Animals talk with delight,
But suddenly I see a croaky frog,
I ask him how he got his croak,
He says spiders jumped down his throat,
I try to search for other frogs,
Then I see a purple river,
There is a frog sitting on it, on a water lily,
He tells me that he is the same frog as before
And that the spiders jumped out of his throat.
Now he does not have a croaky voice,
It is back to normal.

Isla Mather (8)
Whirley Primary School, Macclesfield

Halloween

H elp, where am I?
A ll around me, I can see
L ots of bats and cobwebs
L urking in the shadows.
O ne frightening pumpkin lights the way
W izards make all the Halloween magic come true.
E verywhere I look there are spirits of Halloween joy
E ven magical yellow dragons can be seen.
N ever go near the monster's cave because there is danger to fear.

Elijah Cockburn (7)
Whirley Primary School, Macclesfield

Magical Creatures

U nder the bright sky, the unicorn can be seen.
N ear the shallow sea is where the unicorn and mermaids meet.
I magination and believing are key to being able to see.
C arefully and quietly, who you approached.
O n a Sunday, the unicorns and mermaids have fun and play!
R unning near the lake, a unicorn sees its own reflection.
N earby, a mermaid was singing a lullaby.

Ella Scragg (8)
Whirley Primary School, Macclesfield

Twilight

T he sky shines bright with one million stars
W hispers of dreams paint cosmic memoirs
I venture through the enchanted woodland
L ingering shadows stay imposing and grand
I n the distance, I see a silhouette
G listening amber eyes, I will never forget
H er stare sends shivers like a cold embrace
T wilight descends revealing the cat's curious face.

Eliza White (9)
Whirley Primary School, Macclesfield

Monsters

M o the monster walked down the street,
O ther monsters, joined him all with smelly, coloured feet.
N ow what will these monsters get up to?
S ome of them went to the zoo,
T he rest of them went to have some fun,
E very now and again one would rest in the sun,
R ound the back more monsters played chase
S o now I think all these monsters are super ace.

Oliver Stuart (8)
Whirley Primary School, Macclesfield

Fast Asleep

I was fast asleep,
Dreaming beautifully,
Of happy days and adventures
In Japan.

Then suddenly...
My dream stopped.
It went dark.

Early in the morning,
Whilst sleeping,
In the dark,
My alarm clock suddenly went *ding, ding, ding!*

I woke up screaming,
Startled, scared,
Then I realised it was time to get up,
A fun time at school day!

Harry Hibberts (9)
Whirley Primary School, Macclesfield

The Upside-Down

I float peculiarly in a strange place,
Back then in the distance I see a familiar face,
"Rob?" I bellow as I am confused,
"Ned?" he responds, as there's no time to lose,
"What are we doing here?"
"Maybe there's someone near?" I say,
So we search and we search until we almost die,
From a giant bird who dives from the sky.

Jack Robson (8)
Whirley Primary School, Macclesfield

My Own Dream

One day I was going to bed,
And I came across a portal.
When I went into it,
I felt like I was immortal.
Every time I stroked a nettle,
It wouldn't sting, so I decided to settle.
I lay myself on a hefty nettle bush,
For some reason, I was in a wheelchair and
Needed someone to give me a push.
When I woke up, I was back in my bed,
I realised it was a dream and
Wondered what was in my head!

Rosa Lampley Spencer (7)
Whirley Primary School, Macclesfield

Monkey And Me

A ball of power came my way
I said, "It's my time, hooray!"
The pigeons squawked and the birds chirped
"Hooray!"
I went to see a monkey and said, "Help me please
I need to save the Dipley Dopley World."
He said, "Hooray!"
My time had come,
"Let's go save the Dipley Dopley World together, yay!"

Coen Beech (9)
Whirley Primary School, Macclesfield

Dreamy Penguins

P enguins slide into my room at night,
E ach in different colours, to my delight.
N ot waddling, but driving trains,
G oing fast in cars and planes.
U nderneath disco lights,
I n the club, they dance all night.
N ow flying high and diving deep.
S ee you next time I go to sleep.

Matthew W (10)
Whirley Primary School, Macclesfield

A Royal Friend

F riendship is her only wish,
R eally hoping that people don't just think of her as rich,
I magine being a princess but still feeling all alone,
E verybody saw her as the one in line for the throne,
N ow at a new school, a chance to be someone new,
D ear reader, could that true friend be you?

Maria Morgan (9)
Whirley Primary School, Macclesfield

When I Race

When I race, I have excellent pace.
When I race, I always come in first place.
When I race, I enjoy the chase.
When I race, I am so ace.
When I race, I embrace the chase.
When I race, I drive into a space.
When I race, I leave no trace.
When I race, I go a pace.
When I race, it's no disgrace
Because I win.

Matthew Cain (9)
Whirley Primary School, Macclesfield

The Corrupted Soul

Darkness swallowed the dead forest,
The undead rose from the underworld,
That thing stalked anything and anyone,
In the distance something appeared,
It sent darkness down the graveyards
To steal what was dead,
That thing limped in the shadows,
Taking lives into hollows,
Nothing was safe,
No one was safe.

Anson Choi (10)
Whirley Primary School, Macclesfield

Dragons

D ragons running away from demons,
R iders meeting to capture them so they can have a switch ride,
A ncient fossils in their den,
G iant dragon protecting its eggs,
O bliterating buildings in one slick,
N oise that will scare 100 people,
S ome getting saved by a smart dragon.

Connor Casey (8)
Whirley Primary School, Macclesfield

The Gymnastics Pony

I went into my garden below the midnight sky
I saw a pony flying so high
It did some magical tricks
And beautiful kicks
As the sun began to rise
The pony told me a big surprise
She told me she was amazing at gymnastics
And I said, "Wow! How fantastic!"
This made me feel so joyful
At how the pony was happy and playful.

Jessica Hooley (9)
Whirley Primary School, Macclesfield

Terror

T he forest is full of trees, eerie silence and a cold breeze.
E yes are searching for their next prey.
R abid fangs are sharp as knives.
R oaming the woodland for its next feast.
O wls lurking in the trees.
R ousing, I woke in a cold sweat. It was back.

Ashley Foster (10)
Whirley Primary School, Macclesfield

Pirate

P irates sail the seven seas,
I n a large ship that moves when the sea does,
R oaming the waters, searching for treasure,
A ttempting to avoid the monster danger,
T owards the island, they go
E xploring the unknown, what treasures will they find?

Riley Scragg (8)
Whirley Primary School, Macclesfield

Grandma

G randma sitting next to me.
R eally happy to see her again.
A beautiful cake she has made.
N ow hugging me really close.
D reams like these are the best.
M orning comes and I am sad.
A n angel in the sky again.

Isaac Jackson (8)
Whirley Primary School, Macclesfield

Daydream

D ancing in the sun
A way with the fairies
Y ou and me together
D istractions blocked
R ainbows shining
E verywhere you look
A magical land awaits
M ade just for you!

Niamh Lee (9)
Whirley Primary School, Macclesfield

Sleepless Dreams

Sleepless dreams, where do you take me?
High up in the sky,
Not to appear to the naked eye,
Will I take a dive?
Making me feel alive,
Revive me from this world,
Emerge from my daydream,
Must seem rather extreme.

Isabelle Whitehead (10)
Whirley Primary School, Macclesfield

Penguin Problems

Penguins panic at the polar,
Arctic antics irritating these Arctic birds,
No more fish on their dishes,
Igloos melting, Arctic grass wilting,
Cracked ice under their feet,
Snow turning to sleet,
Major penguin panic!

Paddy Considine (10)
Whirley Primary School, Macclesfield

Untitled

D ancing in the moonlight,
R eaching for stars that gleam,
E thereal whispers,
A world of possibilities,
M oments woven in a seamless seam.

Samuel Mather (11)
Whirley Primary School, Macclesfield

Scary

S omething lurking in the dark,
C reepy noises,
A round me shadows form,
R unning, always running,
Y awning, awake, I burst into tears.

Eve Lewis (10)
Whirley Primary School, Macclesfield

Sonic

S onic Dream Team is my dream
O n a Green Hill
N ext to Tails, running at the speed of sound
I nto a loop-de-loop
C hemical plant next.

Spencer Davies (7)
Whirley Primary School, Macclesfield

I Just Want To Wake Up!

I ran along the grass so green,
Suddenly, I felt as light as a bean,
Floating along as fast as a cloud,
Until I plummeted to the ground.

I landed on a frying pan,
Argh, I was being cooked by my nan!
She was making me into a delicious pancake,
And I started sizzling like a steak.

Nan tossed me up into the sky,
And I landed in a pool in sunny Dubai,
Relaxing on a lilo in the hot sun,
Sipping on a slushie, until I heard, run!

I was shaking in my skin,
As I saw a shark with a pointy fin,
A shark as large as the Titanic,
Luckily, as his mouth began to open,
I woke up in a panic.

Hari Griffiths (10)
Ysgol Gynradd Gymunedol Gymraeg Llantrisant, Miskin

Dream Destination

I have a dream kind of thing,
Something like Martin Luthor King,
The world would be a better place,
If everyone had a dream to chase.
To be a rockstar, shining bright,
Or a gymnast, super light,
An astronaut shooting up to space,
Perhaps a celebrity famous for a race?

But my dream is to dance!
I can express myself when I prance,
Show the world the real me,
Twirling, leaping, stretching to see,
What I can achieve with a focused mind,
A little happiness to mankind.
I may not be as great as Mr King,
But this is what makes my heart sing.

Freya Parry (11)
Ysgol Gynradd Gymunedol Gymraeg Llantrisant, Miskin

Picture-Perfect Dream

Once upon a time I had a dream,
One that was perfect for me.
I see me standing in a room,
A picture-perfect room.
A paintbrush and a palette in my hands,
Drawing a picture of other lands.

I use many colours,
Yellow, purple, pink,
But all of a sudden,
I spill my drink.
And right in front of me is a masterpiece,
The world's best art piece.

Now I know that's just a dream,
And it's my head playing with me.
But I will make it true,
Just watch and see,
Because this is my,
Picture-perfect dream.

Celyn Stephens (11)
Ysgol Gynradd Gymunedol Gymraeg Llantrisant, Miskin

My Perfect Dream

My perfect dream,
The best dream by far,
Is to play rugby for Wales,
And be a Welsh star.

To walk out of the tunnel,
To the sound of the crowd,
Sing the National Anthem,
And make my family proud.

After the whistle,
I'll score the first try,
The crowd will be singing,
I'll be on a high.

We win the game,
My teammates and me,
We win the World Cup,
And the Webb Ellis trophy.

This is my dream,
The best dream by far,
I'll work hard to achieve it,
And be a Welsh star.

Osian Williams (11)
Ysgol Gynradd Gymunedol Gymraeg Llantrisant, Miskin

The Forgetful Dream

My dreams feel so real,
I can't believe it, it's unreal,
In the night or in the day,
Doesn't matter, but it makes me want to stay,
I wake up tired every morning,
And forget my dream without any warning,
I walk to school, very puzzled,
And think and think until I struggle,
I feel so dumb and stupid,
It's like I've been excluded,
I don't care how long it takes,
I wish I never made mistakes,
Hopefully, one day I will remember,
I will think and won't surrender.

Mari Jones (11)
Ysgol Gynradd Gymunedol Gymraeg Llantrisant, Miskin

Jake The Snake

Hello, hello?
Jake had landed somewhere,
Somewhere where nothing was fair,
He felt sick,
Jelly legs,
But somehow everything was slick.

The colours were blending,
Blending blue and purple,
But nothing was fair,
So it was so hurtful,
He looked around,
So many creatures.

Then he saw a snake,
He said his name was Jake,
He was nice, very nice,
He was slithering along,
He let me come,
Come for an *adventure*!

Lucas Gilligan (10)
Ysgol Gynradd Gymunedol Gymraeg Llantrisant, Miskin

Black Cat

I was walking around,
Around my school grounds,
And then I realised,
I had long black ears,
Obviously, so I could hear,
And a long weird tail,
I had four legs and yellow eyes,
I think I looked nice,
I was a black cat,
And then I awoke,
I could smell smoke,
My breakfast was ready.

Molly Wheel (11)
Ysgol Gynradd Gymunedol Gymraeg Llantrisant, Miskin

Am I Dreaming?

Am I dreaming? Is this real?
I am sitting with a dolphin, having a meal.

Am I dreaming? This can't be right!
I am watching a lion and a hedgehog fight.

Am I dreaming? I don't know!
I am watching a turtle sunbathing in the snow.

Now I'm awake, what a night!
I look outside, and... is that a cat with a kite?

Kienan Noble (11)
Ysgol Gynradd Gymunedol Gymraeg Llantrisant, Miskin

A Dream Like Something

A dream like no other,
As I walk on the clouds,
A monster appears,
And all the candyfloss,
But it eats it all,
But I fly across the Earth of dreams,
I love it,
But it's time to go,
Back to my world of hope and joy,
But I will come back to my dream home.

Kimmi Kenny (11)
Ysgol Gynradd Gymunedol Gymraeg Llantrisant, Miskin

YOUNG WRITERS INFORMATION

We hope you have enjoyed reading this book – and that you will continue to in the coming years.

If you're a young writer who enjoys reading and creative writing, or the parent of an enthusiastic poet or story writer, do visit our website **www.youngwriters.co.uk**. Here you will find free competitions, workshops and games, as well as recommended reads, a poetry glossary and our blog.

If you would like to order further copies of this book, or any of our other titles, then please give us a call or visit **www.youngwriters.co.uk**.

Young Writers
Remus House
Coltsfoot Drive
Peterborough
PE2 9BF
(01733) 890066
info@youngwriters.co.uk

youngwriterscw